All Scripture references taken from the KJV of the Holy Bible, unless otherwise indicated.

The Unseen Life
by Dr. Marlene Miles

Freshwater Press 2024

freshwaterpress9@gmail.com

ISBN: 978-1-963164-62-6

Paperback Version

Table of Contents

The Unseen Life

Freshwater

I was not born perfect, yet had it not been for the imperfections there would be nothing to write about. Had there not been imperfections nothing would have happened. And if nothing had happened, there would have been nothing to tell. Oh, but there is so much to tell.

No one wants to hear about perfection. Perfection is boring, especially to the *imperfect.*

Perfection makes enemies of the imperfect, and it draws enemies who are also imperfect. Not only that, but those enemies are also often the violent types. They are stealthy, surreptitious and they come to steal, kill, and destroy, by any means necessary--, even by spiritual violence which can provoke and foster physical violence.

They are spiritual enemies that inhabit physical bodies that are not their own. They appear as interlopers and squatters, but they are either invited or have tricked their host into allowing them or keeping them there. They have no concept of time, so like bad guests, once there they don't leave unless you **make** them leave.

Spiritual enemies are invisible, so even if your eyes are looking right at the person who means you violence and harm, it is difficult to see because it is most often someone you know. And often it is someone you trust, or have trusted in the past, and maybe never should have trusted. Like ever. But because of the invisibility of spiritual enemies, the flesh person that you are looking at in the natural, is blamed for the thing that spiritual interlopers are doing.

Truthfully, humans still must take responsibility for their own actions, but with Wisdom and discernment we should be able to see the spiritual issue behind the natural manifestation. In that way, we are not to take any fights into the physical with that person. We are to remain spiritual, basically, when dealing with the unseen realm.

That person is acting out or walking out unseen evil; most victims never see it coming. That person is walking out unseen violence, that person may be walking out spiritual violence which most often is invisible, but it does impact the physical realm, grievously so, sometimes.

Violence does the opposite of creating, violence kills. Even though, since the times of John the Baptist the Kingdom of Heaven has suffered violence, Christians have authority to also use violence to defend ourselves from loss, and to take back what has been taken from us, by Force.

Why since the times of John the Baptist and not since before then?

That is because even though there was a lot of violence *before* John the Baptist, it was not until men got saved and baptized that they could employ Godly violence to defend and recover their lives, their possessions, and their destinies.

Cain was not born perfect; there was so much sin in him that he killed his brother. I am not saying that Abel was born perfect, but certainly more obedient than Cain. Even so, Abel had no recourse to take back what Cain took from him; but we do. We have Jesus Christ, and we have the Holy Spirit of God. And even though the Spirit of God is Holy, He is not a pushover.

Be ye holy; for I am *holy*.
(1 Peter 1:16)

Holy means hallowed, consecrated, or set apart to a sacred use, or to the service or worship of God. Certain days are *holy* unto the Lord such as the sabbath. We use *holy* oil. We, the saints of God are supposed to be aware that we are the temple of the Holy Spirit and be *holy* vessels as much as it is in us to be. Collectively, we are set aside as a *holy* nation, a royal priesthood, often indicated as a *holy* priesthood. The place where God resides is called the *holy* temple. Things used in service and worship are often consecrated and set aside for that one purposeful use only and those things are called *holy*.

God's laws are *holy* and are therefore called *holy* laws.

And in your Unseen Life, which many may think that you are in stealth mode and no one can see the sins and egregious things you may do, there is always a great cloud of witnesses. Nothing you did is under the radar.

You and your acts and deeds are fully on the radar. God has *holy* witnesses everywhere. *You* may be the reason why there is radar in the first place.

God is not the only One keeping an eye on you. The devil has *monitoring spirits* and *familiar spirits* spying on the saints of God every chance he gets. You're a star, and whether you do well or you do evil there is a spotlight on you, if not in the natural, then in the spirit.

If you were an actor in training and a line was given to you, you may ask the writer or the director, *What is my **motivation***? *What is my reason for saying this, doing this, or being like this?* By Unseen Life, I mean the motivation that causes you to do or say anything may be hidden to you---, you are just doing what is in the *Script* of your life, taken out of the volume of the book where it is already written of you.

(We will talk more about that later.)

The Cloak of Zeal

When the righteous suffer violence and the violent take it by force our Godly passion for the endeavor of taking, taking back, or restoring something that has been taken from us is called holy zeal.

For the zeal of thine house hath eaten me up; and the reproaches of them that reproached thee are fallen upon me. (Psalm 69:9)

Righteous indignation can compute to zeal. This zeal moves a man past passion to having a great drive, verve, or enthusiasm in pursuit of a Godly outcome. Righteous anger is not personal anger, it is an overarching feeling for a collective, for the greater good of a group or people. Godly anger, hating what God hates with perfect hate can lead to zeal, this is on the Lord's side, of course because we are talking about righteous zeal. Passion makes a man do things that he might not otherwise do. Passion or zeal may drive a man to do something that he may not actually know how he happened to do that thing; it was as though he was driven.

Since the times of John the Baptist, the violent will take things, or take things back, by force. Zeal can lead to battles and wars. Righteous anger can lead to *holy* wars, that is wars sanctioned or approved by God.

The Lord is a man of war; the Lord is His name. (Exodus 15:3)

Wars that people fight that involve God are considered *holy* wars. Of course, no one should ever undertake a battle or go to war without first seeking God. And they shouldn't go without first counting up the cost of that war.

For he put on righteousness as a breastplate, and an helmet of salvation upon his head; and he put on the garments of vengeance for clothing, and was clad with zeal as a cloak.

According to their deeds, accordingly he will repay, fury to his adversaries, recompence to his enemies; to the islands he will repay recompence.

So shall they fear the name of the LORD from the west, and his glory from the rising of the sun. When the enemy shall come in like a

flood, the Spirit of the LORD shall lift up a
standard against him.
(Isaiah 59:17-19)

When God says, *Pursue and overtake them*, or *Go and conquer, take the land, possess the land, possess your possessions*, or *Totally destroy the enemy*, that war has been sanctioned by God and can be termed a *holy* war. Make no mistake about it, taking it by force is a war. Short-term, or long-term, it doesn't matter—if force is involved, it is a war.

Wars always involve deities of some kind because people fight wars over what they believe in, and especially when what one side believes in doesn't jibe with what the other side believes in. In so doing each side has their own deity or deities. They each have their own "god" or "gods."

Wars are always spiritual whether folks believe it or not. All wars are not *holy* because **only God is Holy**, but wars are spiritual. So, in tribal wars where one tribe is fighting another for safety, or land, or water rights, or anything, if Jehovah God is not in it – there is no way it can be called holy because little g "*gods*" are not holy.

There is none holy as the LORD: for there is none beside thee: neither is there any rock like our God. (1 Samuel 2:2)

The New Baby Smell

I was not born perfect, but who could tell? Parents are often seduced with the idea of, the perceived innocence of, and the *new baby smell* of the new life form entrusted to them. You'd think we'd all figure out that one day that perfect newborn will become a no-shouting 2-year-old, an absent-minded grade schooler, perhaps a self-involved preteen and *whatever* kind of teenager that may get on their parents' last nerves.

Still, imperfect newborns who are perceived as perfect, keep coming into the world, and are welcomed by loving parents.

I was not born perfect. But my parents probably couldn't, and probably didn't want to know, think, or tell otherwise. No one in my immediate environment could tell, because those who are **also not perfect** cannot discern imperfections, perfectly, or sometimes at all--, although some try exhaustively. Parents are not willing, even when they are asked to, or even when pressured, to discern or disclose the imperfections of their child or children.

New baby? Old foundation. What does your old foundation *smell* like? Will that delightful smell override the hopes and joys and smells of the new baby that was just born into your family, or into your bloodline? We all certainly hope so, but it takes so much more than hope.

You cannot put new wine into an old wine skin. According to studies the new wine will cause the old skin to burst. But we welcome new babies to Earth every day and they come here into the "skin" of their bloodline; they come here into the foundation of a bloodline, and foundations are ancient, they are old.

What will happen now? What will happen to that baby that is now born into a particular bloodline with a particular foundation?

Entropy

I keep telling you, I was not born perfect. Had I been, there would be nothing to write about. Neither were you born perfect, nor any new baby that is cute as all get out and even has the new baby smell that is so inviting to adults.

The reason none of us were born perfect is because we each were conceived, shaped and born according to the foundations of our bloodlines. Where is there a perfect man? That man has a perfect spiritual foundation. Where is there a faithful man? That man has a perfect foundation. Where is there a righteous man? Well, that man either has a perfect foundation, or God, by Grace, Mercy and faith has counted that man righteous by the Blood of Jesus.

The reason that has to be done is because of the chaos that is found in any natural man's *spiritual* foundation. Foundation is a spiritual matter. Jimmy's mom and dad could be the best looking, the smartest, the richest, and nicest people. Jimmy could have been born into millions or billions and his education and career is fully established and waiting for him to grow into it--, that's all in the natural.

But what of Jimmy's folks' spiritual makeup? Is it ordered or disordered? Is there chaos and entropy in it?

Scientists say that the entropy of the universe is increasing, therefore being born perfect would be newsworthy if it were at all possible. No one is born perfect, well not since Adam and Eve, except one--, Jesus Christ. Perfect means physically whole and spiritually sound and full of the Holy Spirit and no other *spirits.*

Because the disorder of the universe is increasing, my entropy should not be more interesting than your entropy or the entropy of the guy next to us. Chaos, entropy, or disorder seem to be the norm rather than the exception.

Disorder means irregularity or confusion. It could also relate to war, chaos, or disturbances in society. Disorder can relate to the environment, or the person's mind, such as a disordered brain, intellect, or reason. It could speak of a diseased or irregular physical being, or spiritual make up.

It is disheartening to think that the entropy or the disorder of the world, spiritually speaking, is getting worse rather than better since man has been set in dominion and authority to do as Jesus did and undo the works of darkness, which are the works of chaos and disorder.

Had I been born perfect; nothing would have needed to happen to me. Nothing would have happened around me, about me, or concerning me. Nothing could have happened; chaos would have been blocked. Perfection will not allow compromise or change, even on Earth. Once a thing is **perfect** it is complete, it is whole, and it resists being tampered with by virtue of its inherent order, or not being disordered.

When that which is perfect is come, that which is imperfect will fade away.

When that which is perfect presents itself, that which is imperfect – that is every imperfect thing **must** fade away because the Word says so, and because there is no way to get to that which is perfect. That which is perfect is also described as holy and there is a shield around it--, nothing imperfect or evil can touch it. If all things are made new and made perfected, then those things that are imperfect that cannot reach the perfect things must fade away because they will have nothing to do, no purpose, no purchase point, no way to alight on or attach themselves to things that are whole and perfect.

Utopia will have been reached.

Until then, we change, we progress, we grow, we matriculate, and we become, physically speaking, but especially spiritually speaking.

Be ye not unequally yoked together with unbelievers: for what fellowship hath righteousness with unrighteousness? and what communion hath light with darkness?

And what concord hath Christ with Belial? or what part hath he that believeth with an infidel?

And what agreement hath the temple of God
with idols? for ye are the temple of the living
God; as God hath said, I will dwell in them,
and walk in them; and I will be their God,
and they shall be my people.

Wherefore come out from among them, and
be ye separate, saith the Lord, and touch not
the unclean thing; and I will receive you.
(1 Corinthians 6:14-17)

What communion does light have with darkness? Can demons hang out with God? Demons can't even get into Heaven, else, all those who participate in works of the flesh would be able to get into Heaven when it is all said and done. But, they will not be allowed entrance.

Shame, really because those who want to indulge in the works of the flesh care so much about what club, what school, what neighborhood they can get into, but do they not realize that entrance into all those swanky places does not guarantee entrance past the Pearly Gates and the Third Heaven in the afterlife.

I've not ever heard one soul say, *Man, I've been trying to get into that church, but there's a waiting list, or you have to know someone to get in there. But I'm willing to wait because I really want to get into that church.*

But a country club or a certain school for their kids? They are all about that acceptance and admission to man-made places.

Scientists say that the disorder of the universe is increasing. What do the *spiritual* men and woman of God say? Is spiritual entropy increasing, or decreasing? Now that we have Christ, are we accepting Christ and walking with Christ more and setting spiritual order in our lives and in our world, or is the devil winning?

Au Secours! Help!

If I had been born perfect, no one would have helped me do anything, and no one would have done anything for me. Of course I would not have needed anything. I would not have thought that I needed to do anything.

As a general rule, people do not care for, or care about people who seem perfect, maybe perfect or on their way to perfection because of having been perfected.

God knows we have all sinned and fallen short. God knows we all need one-another ministry. God given gifts unto men for mankind and instructed us to be our brother's keeper and look out for one another. So many times, we need the truth in love when we can't see things that are hidden to us that are keeping us from progressing in life.

God sits high and looks low—Jesus walked among the people. Jesus was the Perfect Man, is that why He seemed to be resisted by many. I don't believe that Jesus flaunted His perfection, but He modeled it for those with eyes to see. Surely it irritated the devil though, especially in the Wilderness temptations, and it surely irritated those with the *spirit of the devil,* or any of the *spirits* that serve the devil.

God perfects those things that concern *His.*

The LORD will perfect that which concerneth me: thy mercy, O LORD, endureth for ever: forsake not the works of thine own hands.
(Psalm 138:8)

There is no reason however that any of us should resist being perfected by God since we are called to be like Jesus.

No one cares for the person who is **not** suffering, in any of the ways that people suffer. So many more do not care for the person who *is* suffering, so much less for the one who is *not* suffering.

Few, if any, care for a person who doesn't have a weight problem or an emotional disorder, a self-esteem issue or some other human foible. No one cares for a person who has no financial needs, especially the person who is financially fit, well-off content, satisfied, rich, or wealthy.

If it can be understood, the person who lacks perfection and needs to be perfected and is seeking perfection and is in the process of being perfected is going *THROUGH*. So, in your humanity, you should look at that person as needing support, emotionally, spiritually, mentally, rather than disdaining them because they already seem to have more than you do.

Yup.

• Pruning

I am the true vine, and My Father is the vinedresser. Every branch in Me that does not bear fruit He takes away; and every branch that bears fruit He prunes, that it may bear more fruit.(John 15:1-3 NKJV)

Some pruning is visible to you and others, some is unseen. The spiritual life that any of us are living may not be seen, but it is still happening, and must happen. Unless the Holy Spirit reveals it to us, we don't really know what any other person is going through.

• Broken Vessel

Then I went down to the potter's house, and,
behold, he wrought a work on the wheels.

And the vessel that he made of clay was
marred in the hand of the potter: so he made
it again another vessel, as seemed good to the
potter to make it.

Then the word of the LORD came to me,
saying,

O house of Israel, cannot I do with you as
this potter? saith the LORD. Behold, as the clay
is in the potter's hand, so are ye in mine hand,
O house of Israel.

If you don't think it hurts to be broken,
then you don't know what being hurt feels
like. We scream if we get a hangnail or a
papercut. Come on, people--, things can hurt
both physically and spiritually.

• Refiner's Fire

Fire burns, it burns off impurities and
dross; surely that doesn't feel good. Some of
that dross on you or in you, you have learned
to love and made work for your life. But, it has
to go if you are to reach perfection, since you,
also were not born perfect.

Even though being broken, being pruned, or being put through the refiner's fire all hurts, we would do better to yield to it, in the Lord, than resist it and make it take longer, or never happen at all.

Pray—

Father, I surrender to being remade by the Potter. I surrender to being pruned to bear fruit, and to bear more fruit. Lord, I surrender to Your Holy Fire that exposes my flaws, burns off impurities, and brings correction and perfection. Your refining Fire is a finishing Fire and it is for my good, for the good of my bloodline and the good of mankind. Thank You, Father, for you chastise and correct those whom You Love and call, son.

In the Name of Jesus.

*Amen*_____

For the person who walks in the favor of God, because that man is perfect, perfected, or perfecting, no need to be jealous because that man has been through. Going through in the Lord is easier than going through because of demonic attacks, but it is still going through. That man, because of his process and his successes, so far, may draw enemies because of **jealousy**. But God shows favor to whom He will. Logically, if God is showing favor to someone, but you don't feel that God is at this time showing favor to you, why would you distance yourself from that favored person? Shouldn't you want to stay in the vicinity so you can learn how that man got favor from God? Shouldn't you want to at least glean from that favor, or is running away from that person because of jealousy a smarter thing to do? In so running, you may end up in the camp of people who are not only disfavored by God, but possibly under God's judgment.

You decide; *choose ye this day.*

For God said to Moses, "I will show mercy to anyone I choose, and I will show compassion to anyone I choose." So it is God who decides to show mercy. We can neither choose it nor work for it.
(Romans 9:15-16)

Many times, when people have reached perfection in some aspect of their life, even if the other aspects are not yet perfect, one can become keenly aware that those who used to be friends are now aloof. I hate to say it, but missing and scattered friends is often the result of jealousy; they can't stand to see you blessed.

But you go through with God, and in the end, you will be blessed. Period.

Pity mongers find this out early as they *mong* for pity and attention. Sympathy mongers know this as they *mong* for sympathy, but to their chagrin find that pity is not to be available to them. Those who are still going through find that their friends are few and far between.

Worse, enemies arrive. Enemies arise. Enemies arrive from out of nowhere, it seems, and sometimes enemies arise from the pool of people that *used to be* friends. Frenemies, fake friends, hostile relatives, and evil human agents show up, triggered by any number of things. If one of those things is perfection, then the enemy just sent someone on a suicide mission, because you can't mess with perfection. God has His hand in perfection; all things have been made good by the Spirit of God. That man has become a *son* of God and can no longer be messed with.

That power, that demon that attempts to hinder that man will die, in the Name of Jesus.

Pride

Now, if I think I've been born perfect, I am deceived. Knowing and admitting to one's imperfections is the work of the Holy Spirit which brings us under conviction so that we can repent, turn from our wicked ways, and the Lord can heal our land. Our land is the physical earth we live on, but it is also ourselves, as we are clay vessels made of earth.

Our land constitutes the very foundation of our foundation. Land is territory. It is territory that you possess, defend, guard, occupy and make good use of. It is the land on which you live and dwell in safety. It is land where you raise your family. And land is a place, a territory that you bequeath to your children as an inheritance. It is part of your legacy. That you took hold of land and kept it and transferred it at the appropriate time is noticed by God.

But, if we are full of pride and do not seek God in any of these steps we could not only lose out, our generations could also lose out. We do not want to be responsible for our *children's* children having nothing, do we?

Pride opposes the work of the Holy Spirit and will keep a man from perfection. Pride does this by making a man believe he is already perfect and anything that is wrong is someone else's fault, not his own.

Pride also shores up, encourages, and supports the works of the flesh and all that will keep a man from being broken by the Lord, pruned by God, and refined in the Finer's Fire.

The man who is not perfected or working toward perfection will find himself attracting more *spirits* like the one that is in him dragging him further down into walking out the evils that are in his Unseen Life. These evils are invisible, hidden, and buried in his spiritual foundation. These evils are why he does the things he does without even intending to do them. These evils are why he is the way he is, rather automatically, without even pursuing any of those sins. It's as though the sins are drawn to him and he is attracted to the sins.

Confidence

Perfection, which is maturity or *completion,* has a reflection. Bold but Godly confidence is envied and hated, as well. As much as perfection is hated, confidence, which is only a reflection of the real thing, is extremely envied.

Unless you can see, and or hear in the Spirit, you may not know that the *spirit of pride* is present or operating in a person, or bloodline for that matter. But one of the outward manifestations is confidence.

Some see confidence as cockiness or arrogance--, it can go that far, but there is no reason not to be confident in who you are, who you are in Christ. What your purpose is, what you are doing, and having faith in God that you shall reach Destiny.

He Who Envies Does Not Love

He who envies does not love. There's a diametric opposition of the two. Envy is a work of the flesh, and caring is a work of the spirit or the heart of man. Compassion cannot happen without the *agape* love of God. *Agape* is a work of the Spirit through the soul of man. Because we are on earth, and that which is natural comes first, when the flesh is working the soul and spirit have to take a back seat.

Because that which is natural comes first.
(1 Corinthians 15:46)

The flesh is natural. In the world in which we live, the flesh has priority. And, that includes works of the flesh.

If a man decides to envy, he cannot also love. If he decides to hate, he cannot also love.

If he decides to do any other work of the flesh, he cannot also love or at the same time fulfill the Fruit of the Spirit.

Man looks on holiness and either decides that he can't attain to that, or that it is so boring, why would anyone ever want to do that?

Man hates perfection so much in others that he envies its reflection, confidence. Yet he wants it for himself; he wants perfection, or at least to appear perfect.

Perfection can only come from God, through God and by God. Whatever aspect of a man's life that he believes is the only thing missing that would make his life complete is certainly not accurate. If it were so then when that man got that thing--, let's say it's money because that's what most people love to ask God for, then after receiving money, that man would become a nice guy. He would become a decent human being. He would be full of love, but most often he's not, he's full of pride. The unprospered, undelivered soul who didn't have money and now suddenly has a lot of money will be full of revenge and hate. He will automatically be full of greed, because it is never enough.

Some people have this problem with ice cream—they want more. There is never enough ice cream…Guilty!. Now they want to get more ice cream and don't share it – hide it in the freezer.

A lot of the times a person's character will show through when they get a little bit of money, and that's why they don't have more. They won't share or give; they will only sequester it away. God knows.

Had I been born perfect, there would be nothing else to say. Had I been born mature, developed, fully grown, I would have been confident, and confidence brings in enemies. Enemies arrive and enemies arise.

Even if I had been born into this Earth perfect, I would not have been perfect because. I would still have one problem. I would still have had at least one problem, an enemy. It is more likely that I would still have had problems, plural--, *enemies*. As said before, perfection is as a shield against enemies, but that is if everyone around you and has access to you is also perfect, else those people can be conduits for enemies, even to you.

What did Job do to draw enemies to himself? Nothing. I don't know if Job was perfect, but there were people around him, connected to him by blood who were not perfect, else Job would not have been making offerings on their behalf every week. One person who really was imperfect was that wife.

So, in your foundation there may not be any enemies, but that doesn't stop evil human agents from trying to send enemies into your life. You know the enemies we talked about earlier, the invisible ones who influence visible enemies. You know, the violent enemies who make the people of God to suffer. You, know the spiritual enemies that influence and inflict spiritual violence on the people of God.

But it is because you are not perfect that the enemies can show up, alight, or linger in your soul. It is because you (and I) are not perfect that we draw more like us to ourselves. Multiplication works to the negative as well as to the positive. Whatever is in us, whatever is in our soul is drawing more like itself to us every day that we don't do something about it. Every day that we either yield to temptation, or don't resist temptations, more of the same will come to us.

Have you ever noticed that if you don't purge your emails daily, or at least often, you get the scummiest, lowest emails imaginable? If the algorithm that governs your email even surmises that you are not there, you are not watching, you are not guarding your inbox, all kinds of junk gets into it. Some of this junk used to automatically go to spam, but now it's not.

Evil *spirits* are that way—you have to **make** those *spirits* bounce or they will accumulate in your soul and in your life. Next thing you know, you're clicking on them, I mean acting like them. They are invisible and unseen, but they make you do things that are seen, and will be noticed and will get you into all kinds of spiritual and physical trouble.

The Image-Driven Life

Yet man has found a way to present himself (or herself) well. I call it the image-driven life. Most people are picture perfect on any given day. Every hair is in place. Make up is beautiful, clothes are crisp and clean. They even arrive in places in immaculate, late-model, detailed cars. Their teeth are three shades whiter than God made them or than three daily cups of coffee stained them. These are the beautiful people presenting their beautiful lives to others who they hope and believe are also beautiful people.

But each of these beautiful people each have their own *Unseen Life*. There is a life in the background, on their screensaver that either they only know about, or they only can see. Some of this is evidenced in things that they do, some is evidenced in things happening in their household they live in, or in their family that no one else knows about.

Some people's *Unseen Life* is hidden to even them. They just know that life is full of strange events, and they don't know why certain things are happening to them. All they know is that they plan to try harder and perhaps by sheer willpower they can will themselves to have success in life.

Some of these things are fully covered up because it would be too embarrassing, too humiliating if others outside the home, outside the family, ever knew that their family was like *this*. So, they step out of their houses in their image-driven make-up, and their image-driven clothes, and in their image driven cars to either feel good about themselves for a little while, or at least not be embarrassed by how rage-filled one of their relatives is as he tears up the whole house at least once a week when he gets drunk. They feel as though they can fit in, even though their little sister has been sent away to have a baby because she's 15, and what will the people *say*? What will they say? Especially at church, since no one is saying who fathered that new baby who should have a new-baby smell, but this family will never know that child because it will be given up for adoption or put into foster care as unwanted.

Still, every hair is in place and the image is on point. While the problem is not even what the family looks like, the problem is that the family has lost its humanity. Not one person in that family was born perfect, but they have convinced themselves that the outward appearance will not only make it seem so, but it will make it so.

It will not.

Even an unsaved family will embrace a new baby and not throw a teenager away, or kick them out of the house. But this family, that believes it is saved, has *lust* in its foundation, *alcoholism* in its foundation, *anger, rage,* and *violence* in its foundation and the fullness of *pride,* both *vain pride* and *selfish pride* in its foundation where they do not either care for one another, or know how to care for one another. So, they trot the boards as they **act** as if they are normal acting out the life they want others to see, but their Unseen Life is directing who they really are.

Without God, there is no hope here. No hope.

The Unseen Life

The mystery of life is that all the while I am living the life that you see, I am also living the life that you do not see, *the Unseen Life.* My perfect or competent life has its shadow. Which life is the real one, and which life is the shadow? You can be the judge, but know that the seen life, the image-driven life can be manipulated. The *Unseen Life* cannot be manipulated, made up, covered up, or masqueraded.

Whether we are also perfect, or imperfect is yet to be seen. There's a life that must be lived behind the scenes, behind what is *seen*, that life has a life of its own.

That life is automatic and driven by unseen forces that are mandated to fulfill roles, scenes, and scenarios.

Had I been born perfect. I would not have had to live also that *Unseen Life* of which I speak. Because *Unseen Life causes* the imperfections that are seen in the *seen* life. I could have just lived the life that is seen. I could have just lived the life of childhood games, playing outside in the yard, of working in the vegetable garden with my dad. It may have included cheerleading in middle school, enjoying college and becoming a working adult.

I could have lived the perfectly ironed and crisp-shirted life with perfect smiles and teeth and welcoming walk-on parts and cameos.

But I was not born perfect. Therefore, the play, the drama, the action behind the **visible** began the day I was conceived, probably, but the lights were not turned on until I arrived in the atmosphere of Earth. The cameras were not focused until my mother, my father and Mrs. Ophelia Washington, my mother's midwife, and God said, *Action,* so all those humans then finally looked on me in the flesh, in the natural.

Action!

Action! was commanded by the director of this trauma, and I took a deep breath and uttered my first line, which was probably crying. Babies are smarter than we give them credit for many times.

Perhaps I should have cried. So, I did.

We are in more than 40 seasons. The ratings? Well, you decide. No show is perfect, remember? But you decide. The imperfect person who is in more than 40 seasons is still here trying. The challenge is, God's way, or the way of the *Unseen Life?* As long as God's way is the way of the unseen, that is where there is victory, success, and prosperity.

If the unseen is not God's way, that means that the enemy is running the show. That mean's that the Script of the Unseen Life does not match what is happening on the stage.

Adam

Why was I not born perfect?

Perfect? By what standard? Perfect by human medical standards--, thank You, Lord. But spiritually perfect can only be in God and of God. Spiritually imperfect can never be God's fault since so many humans since Adam have been involved in and had input in my being here and with the foundation that I now have.

Only Adam and Eve (before the fall) and Jesus were Perfect because God was their foundation, not men. So, there would be no need to do work on my foundation or correct any matters that concern me if I were Adam, Eve, or Jesus. Yeah, that kind of perfect.

Too many of us think that if we don't do things to people, then they won't do things to us. Wouldn't that be nice, if that was the case?

The answer was clear. Adam, and everyone that came after Adam, all the way up to my mother and father, but especially my mother and father and especially their mothers and their fathers hold the keys to why I was not born perfect.

Why was I not born perfect? There are reasons. Three reasons.

- One, the *Unseen Life*.
- Two, flesh bodies get old and wear out.
- And the third reason, was that I was born at all. It was by God's Grace and Mercy that even though I would not be born perfect, there would be hope and Grace and opportunity to become a *son* of God and become perfect, spiritually speaking, in His eyes, and that God would see me as one of the Righteous by the Blood of Jesus.

Even though perfection was not part of my description at my birth, innocence was, thank God, but also because of God's Grace and Mercy. I was born into the Earth in spite of the Law of Sin and Death being in place. Therefore, I am given a chance--, an entire lifetime to get it right before a Righteous God.

So, I was not born perfect, but I was born. And that right there is a miracle and also a testimony.

Scene 1

The first cry was only *my* debut. The drama had already begun.

William Shakespeare said. *The world is a stage, and everyone plays their part.* My **part** began many years ago and I still play it today. If I'm typecast, I don't know. I believe that I will remake my character over from day-to-day. Every day. I believe I'm original and have fun doing it--, but what if I'm not?

If I am original, it confuses people. It confuses enemies, both that I choose to restyle often. And that I *can.* Amazing, His Grace.

Originality confuses people, especially followers. Originality confuses, especially *blind followers*. Originality brings enemies. More enemies? Yes.

Why?

Enemies, when they think they've finally got you figured out, but then they find they can't figure you out. If they only knew that in my imperfection, I can't figure myself out, somedays; and so, I've stopped trying.

Originality takes vision. If a life is unseen obviously there is no vision. Without vision, the people perish is what the Word of God says. Careful, saints of God.

You do know that this is an imperfect world of imperfect people, most of whom can barely figure anything out, least of all themselves and most of all other people.

What Part Am I Playing?

You are playing the part that is your part – unless you try to acquire someone else's role. That is ill-advised, but many try it.

But back to the drama of the Unseen Life.

What part am I playing?

My part. Me. It's the only part that I can play. It is the only part one can play with ease, clarity, and assurance.

Unless I remake myself over and over again, I will fall prey to the other actors on the stage as they try to figure out who I am and consciously or unwittingly try to either *become* me, or undo me. Not so much that I'm wonderful, but it is that I am someone they can look at and see. Unless they choose to look at and see *themselves* becoming *themselves* over and over again. Isn't it human nature to study others, complaining about the splinter in another's eye and ignoring the log in your own?

I recently was told all kinds of things that I did when I entered a building and then left it, that I never did. How was this possible? Someone or some ones were studying me, instead of being themselves and doing what they were supposed to have been doing that day, in that building.

My splinter, or your log – you decide.

I say this because those who are walking out the image-driven life and desperately trying to suppress the Unseen Life will surely never balance anything. The Unseen Life cannot be suppressed, it can only be attempted to be covered by another life that is seen in the physical to other people. So are you being true to your Unseen Life and trying to work it out and improve it, correct matters that concern you, for real?

Or, are you faking it, hoping that you will make it any how? Make it where? I don't know--, into the country club, that exclusive subdivision, that certain college or university. But even if you do, once you get there, your Unseen Life will still be raging.

The cue is given; you walk out on the stage of the scenes that you are supposed to play out today. Today, will you *become*, or let God help you to *become*, **or will you stay in costume and makeup and remain an** *actor* **in your own life?**

The Righteous Judge is watching. Ask Him what <u>He</u> wants you to *become*, then *become* that, even if you only become it a little at a time, day by day. You still *become* it.

Once you become it; it becomes you. It adorns you; it glorifies you. Your becoming who and what you are designed and destined to become is becoming and makes you attractive to both God and all other people who you will meet in this lifetime.

Everybody is a star or should be. Really everybody *has* a star, unless it has been moved, raided, stolen, covered, or otherwise obfuscated by the enemy. I say you're a star because you too, have a part in this drama that is your life. In so doing, you also play a part in the lives of many others.

Be yourself; you, do you and let me be me.

Characters

Here come the characters, the characters of the Unseen Life cast into humans who are born, who have already cried with the midwife or doctor and are walking, sleepwalking, almost dozing or doing the zombie walk on the stage of their *Unseen Life.* Even though I am not inclined that way, I'm not bent that way. The other actors do not know it and still walk on the stage on cue with their costumes, makeup and lines prepared, many not knowing what or why-- they just do it. They just do it because the Script of the Unseen Life compels them. And propels them out onto the stage.

What brings them onto the stage right on cue? Their foundation. Their blood. Their Script, written by their ancestors hundreds of years ago, and compiled by many more since then. Their sin, their iniquity, their purpose, their destiny all bring them out onto the stage. It is a complex juxtaposition of good and bad entanglements that draw or push a person in one direction or the other. It is unseen, but it is. And, it is very powerful.

Your great-great somebody did not swim, but they always wanted to. Time passed and they died.

Here you come along in your generation. You didn't even know the tide was coming in that day. Or that the ocean ebbed and flowed, or that there was a cycle to it. You did not know that the ocean and all of Creation also play a part in the Unseen Life.

Your great grandfather and your grandfather always dreamed and daydreamed of swimming, but neither of them did it. Your grandfather always wanted to swim but could not because he was not supposed to. His *kind* couldn't swim in the pool or sun on the beaches abutting the ocean. Maybe they couldn't *float; m*any of those kinds can't. Your father did swim, but only once, and no one found out except his wife, and she covered it up until this very day.

Why is this water pursuing you as it were, even if you had no part to play. You, with no desire to swim, or play the part of a person who swims, have wandered on stage or a dramatic set where there is a pool or an ocean. Why do you love the water and keep going to the beach? It is your Unseen Life. You have been called and charged to fulfill the things that your great-great could not and did not. Even the mundane things that have been put into your foundation, and thereby written in your Script.

It's Not What It Looks Like

It's not what it looks like. I keep telling you **it's not what it looks like.**

You may be wondering, or exclaiming, *"I don't know why this happened or keeps happening to me. I don't know why this water is pursuing me."*

The water is pursuing you because your great-great somebody wrote it into the Script that is tucked away between two rocks or two walls of your foundation and someone in his bloodline must do this swimming thing because great-great wanted desperately to do it, but he did not. Great-great may not have spoken it to a soul or told anyone else at all, not even God, but his very soul wrote it in the foundation of his bloodline because he could, because he was the patriarch and could encode for the bloodline, whether he knew he had that much power and could do that, or not.

Wishes. Dreams. Thoughts. Daydreams. Wants. Yearnings. This is another power of the soul, even if the person struggles to repress what he wants to do. If he has idols or idol *gods* and they are influencing him to be curious about a thing, yet he resists and never acts on them, if he is not delivered of that idol, or that devil, then that spirit can write on that man's foundation.

Let it be written. Let it be written that this man wants to swim.

To a spiritual entity that man is his entire bloodline. To God, in the Spirit that man is his entire bloodline. To God YOU are your entire bloodline, not that they will be finished as a bloodline, but the last part that is written of you will be written of the last person in your bloodline and all that come in flesh and walk this Earth in between you and eternity.

Foundation is why little Johnny suddenly comes into the family and he is so different --- good or bad, than the rest of the kids. It is encoded in the foundation that one of these kids will be a swimmer. Whether it is decided that it is the first, the second, the boy, the girl, or the 5th generation is not known, until it is known. It is in the foundation; therefore, it is in the blood.

Saints of God, might this give you a clue as to why Blood is Thick? Blood has a lot of information in it, both medical, physical, and spiritual information.

We pray that your great-great was indeed great in a positive way and didn't send or leave great battles for you and your life.

You may say, *really?*

Some of the stuff left for me to play out was left by my mother, father, grandparents, and great-grandparents.. And so was the stuff that you, so far have been and are to play out left for you. Leftovers, possibly. Probably.

Leftovers are left in a foundation. The foundation of a family … is the blueprint that that bloodline is to walk out or is likely to walk out if they don't do something different, spiritually speaking. There are left turns and right turns in walking out a bloodline blueprint. Left turns are to the dark kingdom, right turns turn a man and his family, his bloodline back to Jesus.

Coming to Earth to play your part is part of your *chores*.

The Unseen Life continues, and you are cast as yourself in the part that must be played.

The only way out is by Jesus Christ. The only way out is a new foundation. The only way out is new blood; the Better Blood, the Blood of Jesus Christ, and a transfusion.

The Director

Will you choose Director One, or Director Two? One or Two? The beauty is you get to pick one, you get to pick who you want to direct as you play the *Unseen Life*, and as you choose to expose or conceal that life by living your seen life right out in front of everyone who has eyeballs in their heads, or living a fake, pretentious life that makes you look perfect. You get to choose, unless the director has already been chosen for you by your parents and your ancestors based on what is already in your imperfect foundation.

Even if they have chosen the director of the dark kingdom, you can override that by selecting Jesus Christ and Salvation in Him. Choose this day which *Director* you will obey.

Without making an active choice, who do you think is directing? Who is coaching the football team? The one who has players on the field. Who is directing the Script of your life? Depends on what characters are on the stage.

You're born, and as imperfect as you are, here are your assignments.

One of the first things you must do is learn the language. Learn to speak. Learn to read and write the new language, the language of your life.

Next, find out who the other characters are. Find out who the other characters are likely to be. Who has walk-on parts? Who has cameos? Who are the long running actors alongside you?

Sadly enough, if one actor gets fired from the production, it doesn't matter because another may not. But usually, one who looks similar will arrive to play that part. And, so it continues.

Sometimes those characters are fake. Sometimes they are in heavy makeup and costumes and should not even be on the stage with you, or on the stage at all. They are just out there ad-libbing or improvising. Well, it's up to you to accept or reject their part in your life, whether it is your real, daytime awake life, or your dream life, or your Unseen Life in dreams that are perhaps covered or wiped. It's still your job even if the Director is not on your side and is not directing things in your favor.

Trust in the LORD with all thine heart; and lean not unto thine own understanding.

In all thy ways acknowledge him, and he shall **direct** thy paths.
(Proverbs 3:5-6, *emphasis, mine)*

The Script

Who's sinned? This man or his parents? What parents? The parents who created the Unseen Life.

> O LORD, I know that the way of man is not in himself: it is not in a man that walketh to direct his steps.
> (Jeremiah 10:23)

Your ancestors have left you a litany of things to do, if they left so much work undone. Not just that they had a bucket list of what they wanted to do, but also there are spiritual things that they haven't done because they didn't know about those things, or how to deal with those things effectively. Those things are in your foundation. They are the chores of your life, that you can now add to the things in your life that you *were* sent here to do.

If those things were placed in the family foundation by sin, they are all the more grievous. Those things are not what they presented to the church folk in the pastor, in any image-driven performances, but the stuff they thought nobody saw~~, the real stuff. That's what has been written in the script of your *Unseen Life*. The stuff that was seen or was deemed acceptable for seeing was the play within the play. It was the scene to cover the real scene, which was the *unseen.*

The Script of the Unseen Life is not anywhere near perfect, else the devil wouldn't have hidden it from you, your parents or your ancestors. I was neither born nor written into perfection, nor you in the script of the *Unseen Life* that resides in our respective family foundations.

Adam and Eve had no drama to play out and they sinned. Adam and Eve had no Script based on an evil foundation or a previous ancestral foundation and they still sinned.

Sin created this Script, for the most part.

Dramas are written by Man; Destiny is written by God.

Born into a house with impregnated air, once the first breath was taken, the Unseen Life was energized and began or *resumed* right alongside the seen life, the visible life for any person--, you, me--, any of us.

Somebody with authority to encode for a family may have wished and wished, and then invited that scene. Wrote it on the pages of the playbook of that family. They may not have lived long enough or had the courage to act it out, but they wrote the script for it in the spirit.

Imagination is the ready pen of the spirit writer.

The sin of Judah is written with a pen of iron, and with the point of a diamond: it is graven upon the table of their heart, and upon the horns of your altars: (Jeremiah 17:1)

Come clean. Who did it doesn't matter at this point, the play is playing.

Stop It

How can you make it stop? Especially if it is what someone in authority desired, or if the same desire lasted for generations or from more than one of the *writers*. That is, if there was **agreement**. Even if the individuals didn't even know each other or ever had a conversation or ever *agreed* on the Script.

The inheritance left is your script. It is the script of your Unseen Life and you're to walk it out, work it out daily.

For Thought

What will you do with your imperfect self, and how will you do what is right without Godly perfection?

Mental Weapons

I've known children who looked like weapons. These children look like the way the mom felt about the dad at the time of conception, or the child looks like the way the father treated the mother during pregnancy, and in early childhood.

At that time, she was either herself around them or her *acting* was so poor that the children became her. How many children have *become* their mothers? Instead of becoming what God says they should become, how many kids have become their parents? Couldn't help it--, it's in the Script, it's in the foundation; it is in the blood of that family.

They've become not the outer show or the outer shell, but the inner life, the secret,

Unseen Life? The darker life that few, if any others really know about.

Yet these children were born to become her allies. These were her secret weapons that she may have been creating. The creation or formation of these weapons may not have been a secret to her. No weapon formed. She may not have even been aware of it herself.

Each of several children looked different, but they each look the way she felt about their father during the early years when she spent the most time with them. Mental weapons soon become real weapons.

Saved people also have unseen scripts that cause them to traipse on the boards of the stage of life.

Eyes of understanding are not opened. Ears are still closed while people hear. People are not discerning habits, traditions, or there is a lack of courage to do something different, or an inability to change. Undelivered, people-pleasers--, any number of reasons why the show of the Unseen Life must go on.

These saved people were also not born perfect, and ever since salvation, have not reached perfection.

Some are blinded by the darkness with no ability to navigate one's way out of it or call for Light.

Even after salvation, some walk out image-driven Scripts that they think they've written, but by the violence in their foundation, they are forced to receive direction from their Unseen Lives.

The woman who loves money is our example. We are warned about the love of and the lust for money. Those who would be rich fall into many snares. The lust for money is the root of all evil.

Now in the Garden there is a tree of life. Therefore, there is a *root* to that tree. The root of good, the root of life.

At the bottom of that tree, buried far beneath the ground, unseen, is the lust of money. That unseen lust causes this woman, many women, many men, to walk the boards of their Unseen Life acting out certain scenes and scenarios.

Here's what that particular root grows.

Whoredoms.   Greed.   Gluttony. Coveting. dissatisfaction. This lady is no whore, but her Unseen Life makes her *look like* a harlot.

Who wrote this script? The *lust* for money in some soul who had authority to write it, wrote it.

As she looks like a whore. Just as there are nice drunks and mean drunks, there are nice whores and mean, serious sex workers. There are nice harlots.

There are mind and soul prostitutes, trading what they believe they have for what they believe they want. There are body prostitutes, those who colonize the red-light district. These are the kinds that we see on racy TV shows and movies. These types wear underwear on the outside. They don't care if their supposed-to-be unseen or unmentionables are seen.

This lady would never set foot in such a place. Or would she? Is there curiosity? we don't know. It's a secret she'd never tell. But all she would do is look, browse, and inquire, perhaps under the pretense or observation, or study. She might even go there unsent, "to pray."

But it's not what it looks like. It's not what it looks like. It never is.

It's not.

No, it's not; it really isn't.

Her Script, written for her by her mother, based on how she felt about her father at the time of this child's conception, birth and early years. Her mother may have often said, *I can raise you all by myself. All I need is money.* Or, *I'm raising you all alone. I sure wish I had more money.*

Money, money, money, Mamma wrote the script. The adult child is living it out.

That lady doesn't have a husband and never had one. Neither did mom. Dad left emotionally, not physically, but he still left.

The mother hated men when she carried and nurtured her oldest girl. So, the daughter's Script, even though she wanted to, and had begun to write her own, instead she began to act out her mother's Script.

She couldn't help it. It's in the blood; it is in that thick, viscous family blood.

When children take on their parents' values, that is, what's important to the mother becomes what is important to the children. What is important to the parents is projected to the child. When even adult children have not established an identity, they must continue the Script left by their ancestors.

The only way to make it stop is Jesus. Except for Jesus, they are locked into it.

The whole world is a stage, and folks with the Scripts of their Unseen Life are stuck on Broadway. Yes, saints, broad is the way that leads to destruction.

Don't be stage struck, run to Jesus and make this invisible, foundational, thick-blooded automation stop.

Dominion

Why can't we see this Unseen Life? Why can't we see any or all of this?

The answer is in why I'm promised a throne. Does it speak of power? Yes, but it speaks of **position**. In position, I can see way over yonder. Although the Wayback Machine doesn't interest me other than to gather information to help me today and tomorrow, I like the other things that I see from this position. On my throne I can see today very well, and I can see tomorrow somewhat. I can see through a glass darkly, but I still can see.

Dominion is a high chair, but it's not for babies.

Babies fall, especially when enemies arrive and arise. They may push one who is not grounded, from his position, and cause a fall.

Unseen enemies arise in the Unseen Life. Unseen enemies are driving the Unseen Life. A position of dominion allows you to see and have authority to remove spiritual enemies, even though they may be unseen. Recall, just because you don't see them doesn't mean that you can't see the results of their having been in your environment.

Sit in Dominion and do your spiritual work.

Don't Play

You can't just quit, although many try to. You can't just take on another part, although many try that as well. You must deconstruct the imperfect Script of a faulty foundation by the power of God. **Prayer and repentance allow God to rewrite your Script.**

It may begin with a name change. If you have a demonic or unfavorable name, no wonder what is happening to you is happening to you. It may change with a scene change, a change of location. God may move you; let Him. Your Script may change when God moves people out of your life or new people into your life—a change of characters. But mostly the change of your Script will be a change in you. God can break you and re-mold you. God can prune you so you will become fruitful or more fruitful. God can put you through the Fire and purify you, or He may do all three. Know that He corrects and perfects those whom He loves. And, whom God loves, He calls, *son*.

If your evil Script is not completely torn down don't wonder why things aren't going well. Still wondering why stuff keeps happening to you or only praying on an as-needed basis will not undo the Script. You may tear out a few pages, but somehow the actors who are supposed to come on cue in those pages will appear anyway. Days, weeks, months, even years of confusion may happen because someone tore out some of the pages.

Rewrite! Author!!! Let God be the Author and the Finisher of your Faith, as well as the Director of your ordered steps and the stage lights of your path.

In your new level, in your perfection you are now no longer in the play of the Unseen Life because your spiritual life and your physical life are reconciled, so there is no longer any play-acting.

> To wit, that God was in Christ, reconciling the world unto himself, not imputing their trespasses unto them; and hath committed unto us the word of reconciliation.
> (2 Corinthians 5:17)

So all that evil coding because of the evil imaginations of your ancestors that created the Unseen Life that you were stuck with living were all trespasses against God. We are to cast down evil imaginations and every high thing that exalts itself against the Knowledge of God. We clearly see one of the main reasons is that that imaginations even if they don't come to pass immediately or in the imaginer's lifetime, they get embedded, encoded, and stuck in the foundation of that bloodline. Then here comes Johnny who has no clue as to what happened, why is he like that, or why do these things keep happening to him.

Put Them Back

I was not born perfect, because I was born on Earth, and I was born a woman by a man. Also, I was not born perfect because of the Unseen Life. My parents were conducting theirs **and I inherited the script**--, their script which *they* inherited.

You would think anything this ancient would be on old, yellowed parchment paper with grayed out ink, but it is not written in the physical, it is written in the spirit. It is written and working by altars that are still alive and emanating, like rumbling volcanoes that seem to erupt underground as not to be discovered. These altars are projecting either for or against you. So nothing has faded if the altars are still being attended to. Nothing has changed and the same cycles that have run through your family and the people in your family are now running through you, as well as making you walk onto the stage and repeat the same old lines and the same old actions as your parents and your ancestors, whether you knew them or not, and get the same results they got--, or worse.

Even if you know them and hate the way they lived and have vowed not to live that way, by sheer will power, you cannot *will* yourself not to speak those lines, and not to do those actions because the Unseen Life is demanding, requiring, forcing you to do it. That is some of the Violence that the Kingdom of Heaven is suffering. Yes, even those who are saved, sanctified, and set aside, unless they've dealt with the altars that are dealing with them, they are walking out the Unseen Life that was scripted by the blessings and cursings of parents and ancestors, possibly all the way back to Adam and Eve.

If you were to acquire a history degree in any country, the time required to earn that degree might vary because some countries are older than others. Some countries have more history, so there is much more to study. Your family has most likely been here for a long, long, time – longer than any historical epoch of any country. All the way back to Adam & Eve? There may be a lot of history and scripting to undo and how is that undone? In prayer.

A New Script

I want a new script. The Lord surely has one for me. Plans of peace. Plans to do me good. Plans of an expected end. Plans of good success, and to do you no harm. A new creation--, a new script, a new life.

The original Script was written by the family's foundation. The foundation is unseen, and it writes the Script for the Unseen Life. The foundation is known as it manifests in the natural, but it is invisible.

Blessed is he who has not seen but has believed.

As children we may embrace or reject doing what our parents tell us to do. But that doesn't matter because you will do what your parents and ancestors tell you to do anyhow, unless there's Jesus. Unless you accept Jesus Christ and do the will of God, become fully converted, you will do what your ancestors and parents tell you to do. You will do what they tell you to do audibly as an obedient child, or you will obey that foundation that has been laid and established for your bloodline even with all of its imperfections built in it.

You will do it because it is in your foundation. You have two choices: choose life, that is in Jesus Christ, or choose death, which is, if you are not already saved is already pre-selected and chosen for you. Even if your parents threatened you with death for disobeying them or tradition, if you don't choose Jesus, yes, even over your parents, you are automatically choosing death.

Choose ye this day, (Deut 28).

He that loveth father or mother more than me is not worthy of me: and he that loveth son or daughter more than me is not worthy of me.(Matthew 10:37)

Herein lies the rub, how do you balance choosing God over your parents without disrespecting your parents? My best answer is that if your natural parents are wrong or in error, and forsake you, the Lord will take you up. In so doing, God, the Father becomes your parent, which is your ultimate goal anyway. But don't be disrespectful to your birth parents when you choose God.

Said another way, you can choose the foundation that you've been born into, or you can choose to build another entire foundation. That new foundation includes new blueprints and creates a new Script for your Unseen Life that you live in the spirit. The Script that tells you where to go, when to go there, and makes divine connections for you as you meet whom you are **supposed** to meet.

The Jesus Script

The Jesus Script has a star--, your star. In that star is your glory, your education, your health, your life, your ministry, your spouse, your children, and your wealth. The Jesus Script has power; in it is your mountain, it has a tree, it has power and purpose; it has destiny.

The other Script, the one you may have discovered already and absolutely hate has none of those things because it has been raided, it has been plundered and it has been ransacked and bankrupted. What's left is scraps, if that for you to try to eke out a living with, and all the while it is trying to drain what little you may still have left of you. This Dark Script gives you barely enough to work, and work, and work as a slave to barely make it to work again another day. This is an Egyptian slavery script... it is the one you are walking out when you go to work and everything you earn goes to bills. This is the Script that you follow when you are exhausted at night when you go to bed, and when you wake up the next morning, you are still exhausted. More than likely, you are also slaving away while you think you're asleep. That is, your body is lying down on your Beauty Rest mattress, but there is no rest and there is no beauty in your life, not even in your dream life.

You need a new Script; you need the Jesus Script.

Born In Sin

I was not born perfect because I was born in sin and shaped in iniquity. My foundation was corrupt; therefore I am not perfect and without Christ I walk an imperfect life following the Script of the Unseen Life, the life that no one sees and no one knows about but me and God. The Script, that if I am not honest, I may lie about--, to myself, to others if I am very prideful, and I may even try to lie to God about it.

Of course that will do me no good, because God is the only one who can help me with this Script problem.

The Script of the Unseen Life may be covered or attempted to be covered up with perfumes, and powders, and fashion and so many affectations that I may deceive even myself into thinking that it doesn't exist.

But it does.

And it will remain until it is dealt with. Not only that if expiration is not called on it, in the dealing with it spiritually, it will live on and my innocent grandchildren and beyond will have to trot out the same scenes of this Unseen Life, wasting time, resources, and purpose in the Earth. In this cyclical madness our bloodline will be threatened.

People are ever clamoring for a son, so their name is not cut off from the Earth. Male or female is not the issue; the issue is what will your bloodline, no matter what it is called--, what will your bloodline reach, attain to, accomplish, or finish as it pertains to why they are here? God will not merely identify your bloodline by your Earth name, He will identify your bloodline by your **blood**.

So, man of God, you get a boy, a male child. And now what? Are you teaching him anything Godly? Are you preparing him spiritually, or just how to primp and preen and look manly, act macho, and talk big? Are you just so excited because you can have your childhood all over again with your male child? Oh please. How is that benefitting your bloodline in the scheme of eternity. That is only a point of pride. God resists the prideful and runs to the humble, those who have humbled themselves under His mighty hand.

A male child with your same last name? Surely, that is mentioned in the Bible, but may I say that as we pray in the Name of Jesus, we are not all named Jesus, or Christ. Yes, there is power in the Name of Jesus, but it is by the Blood of Jesus that He is known and that we are also known to be in Covenant with Him.

Your blood is thick with DNA and other markers that will always identify you to the Father. You'd do better to minister to your natural children spiritually because of their blood that is your same blood, rather than celebrating their genitalia--, which by the way --, no flesh is leaving this planet.

How to Get A New Script

- Get saved.
- Repent.
- Get adopted by God through Jesus Christ.
- Ask God for a new Script.
- Heal your spiritual foundation.

We all know that witchcraft and occultic can throw monkey wrenches into things, even into our foundation. This book has primarily been about the foundation that you were born with, not what anyone has done to you. If you properly deal with the foundation that you have been born into, you will find that no curse can alight in a healed foundation. You will find that you do not attract the foolishness that an unhealed foundation attracts. You will find that the enemy cannot get into a sound

foundation, just as in a building in the natural-
-, there can be no undermining if the
foundation is properly underpinned. Let Jesus
be your foundation. Let Him be the
cornerstone and let Him be the capstone. Be
sealed by the Holy Spirit and live a victorious
life in Christ.

AMEN.

Foundation Prayers

Lord, forgive me for my sins, the sins of my parents and my ancestors, in the Name of Jesus.

I plead the Blood of Jesus over these prayers.

Holy Spirit Fire, fall, in the Name of Jesus. (X3)

Thank You, Lord, for silencing the enemies that attacked my destiny, in the Name of Jesus.

Lord, You said in Your Word that a man can have whatsoever he says; today I come against the Words of my ancestors that have built a faulty foundation that I have inherited, in the Name of Jesus.

Lord Jesus, have mercy upon me and forgive me and my bloodline of the sins that cause iniquity, in the Name of Jesus.

Lord, forgive me, release me from ancestral iniquity that has flooded my foundation, and let me rise and shine, in the Name of Jesus.

Lord, You said when the enemy shall come in like a flood that you will raise up a standard against him; Father raise up a standard against the flood of imaginations that have colored and miscolored my foundation in the Name of Jesus.

Blood of Jesus, speak favor to my foundation, in the Name of Jesus.

Blood of Jesus flow in my foundation and cleanse it of impurity, in the Name of Jesus.

Holy Ghost Fire, sweep through my foundation and cleanse it, refine it, purify it, in the Name of Jesus.

Fire of God, enter my foundation and chase every evil stranger that inhabits it away, no matter how or when they got there, in the Name of Jesus.

Lord, let anything, foolish, fruitless, and unproductive, and sinful that is in my foundation be washed away so that it doesn't affect me, in the Name of Jesus.

Lord, boldly go, deeply go into the foundation of my life, and heal it, in the Name of Jesus.

Lord my Father, break my foundation down and remold it, in the Name of Jesus.

Lord, my foundation needs deliverance. Let it be delivered of every evil stranger, and every evil arrow that is lodged there, in the Name of Jesus.

Lord, my foundation needs deliverance. Let it be delivered of witchcraft captivity, in the Name of Jesus.

My Lord, speak goodness and Mercy to my foundation, in the Name of Jesus.

Lord, silence and kill witchcraft powers that hang around my foundation for evil, in the Name of Jesus.

Lord, cure every sickness and disease hovering in my foundation, in the Name of Jesus.

Lord, uphold my foundation to let it be as <u>You</u> intended it to be, in the Name of Jesus.

Lord, break every evil assignment for me and my generations that is in our foundation, in the Name of Jesus.

Lord, every idol in my foundation demanding worship, I demand that those idols go, go, go--, get out of my foundation, and my life, in the Name of Jesus.

Every wicked coven, council, court, and assembly against my foundation, scatter by Fire, in the Name of Jesus.

Powers that vow that my foundation will not favor me, die with your vow, in the Name of Jesus.

Wicked souls that vow to trouble me through my foundation, I declare and decree that your vow has expired--, now *you* expire--, die, in the Name of Jesus.

Anything growing on my foundation that my Father didn't put there, be uprooted by Fire, in the Name of Jesus.

Evil umbrella that disallows heavenly Light upon my foundation, catch Fire and roast to ashes, in the Name of Jesus.

Evil umbrella blocking Showers of Blessings from God to drop on my foundation for breakthroughs, East Wind of God, tear it to pieces and blow it away, in the Name of Jesus.

Magnet of darkness that attracts failure, frenemies, false people, fake friends, and improper suitors to my foundation, break to pieces, and scatter, in the Name of Jesus.

Anything siphoning goodness from my foundation, be torn asunder and scatter, in the Name of Jesus.

Wicked prophecies and evil imaginations against my foundation, backfire, in the Name of Jesus.

Ungodly and evil imaginations and machinations placed in my foundation by unwise ancestors, be flushed out by the power in the Blood of Jesus. I am in Christ now.

Satanic rope, ties, or any bindings used to tie my foundation down, break to pieces, in the Name of Jesus.

Anchor of backwardness that holds my foundation to one spot and makes me keep repeating evil cycles, break, in the Name of Jesus.

Angel of Darkness, designed to turn my life upside down, catch Fire and roast to ashes, in the Name of Jesus.

Foundational inheritance problems in my life, break, in the Name of Jesus.

Multiple networks of automatic arrows firing at my foundation, backfire, and Fire on your senders, in the Name of Jesus.

Every poison in my foundation, dry up and be of no effect in my life, in the Name of Jesus.

Evil clocks, calendars, and timelines that have reset my foundation, be removed, and explode in the face of your sender, in the Name of Jesus.

Every witchcraft power that vows to destroy my foundation in the spirit, die, in the Name of Jesus.

Every witchcraft or occultic power that vows it will not let me go, die, in the Name of Jesus.

Every wickedness opposing my foundation and my destiny in the spirit, die, in the Name of Jesus.

Every power that exposes my foundation to danger, die, in the Name of Jesus.

Every evil pot that holds my foundation captive, break, in the Name of Jesus.

Every evil hand planting wickedness in my foundation, wither permanently, in the Name of Jesus.

Any urine poured on or excrement placed on my foundation in the spirit to make people hate me, be of no effect against me, dry up, and be blown back in the face of the one who placed it, in the Name of Jesus.

Every evil arrow fired into my foundation, backfire to sender, in the Name of Jesus.

Every arrow of automatic failure causing financial crises in my life, backfire, in the Name of Jesus.

Every arrow of marital failure fired into my foundation so that I've experienced marital failure, backfire, in the Name of Jesus.

Every evil arrow of barrenness and unfruitfulness fired into my foundation and life, backfire 7X against the sender, in the Name of Jesus.

Every arrow of the emptier, waster, devourer, or destroyer, sent against me and my foundation, return to sender 7-fold, in the Name of Jesus.

Any evil animal sent and living in my foundation, eating up good things in my life, come out and die, in the Name of Jesus.

Season of war and adversity in my foundation, END, in the Name of Jesus.

Seasons of Peace, prosperity, and rest, in my foundation, BEGIN, in the Name of Jesus.

Evil powers of my father's house that vows to pull down my foundation, your time is up, die, in the Name of Jesus.

Evil powers of my mother's house that vows my foundation shall not work for me, die, in the Name of Jesus.

Evil powers of my in-laws and exes' houses that vow that they will destroy my foundation, you shall fail; die, in the Name of Jesus.

Witches assigned to cater evil food to my foundation, die, in the Name of Jesus.

Everything against my foundation, die, in the Name of Jesus.

Sorrow promoters, leave my foundation alone and die, in the Name of Jesus.

Lord, I decree favor, and deliverance to my foundation, in the Name of Jesus.

My foundation, I bless you now, in the Name of Jesus.

> Behold, I was shapen in iniquity; and in sin did my mother conceive me. (Psalm 51:5)

Lord, let me see truth, speak truth, be truth and walk in truth in the inward parts, in the Name of Jesus.

Lord, do not let me deceive myself, in the Name of Jesus.

Lord, make me to know Wisdom regarding the parts of me that are even hidden to myself, in the Name of Jesus.

Lord, give me the courage to respectfully identify the parts of my foundation that I must reject, the parts that my ancestors built incorrectly or in error, in the Name of Jesus.

Lord, break me where I need to be broken and put me back together correctly again, in the Name of Jesus.

Lord, break my foundation where it needs to be broken and put it back together in Righteousness, in the Name of Jesus.

Lord, prune me where I need pruning, so I may bear much fruit, more fruit, and fruit that remains, in the Name of Jesus.

Lord, take me and my foundation through Your refining Fire so that impurities and dross will all be removed from me and my foundation, in the Name of Jesus.

Lord, purge me with hyssop, and I shall be clean. Wash me to be whiter than driven snow, in the Name of Jesus.

Father, make me to hear joy and gladness in You because of a righteous foundation and a reconciled spiritual Script that matches who I am in the natural, that You be glorified, Amen.

Lord, hide thy face from my sins, and blot out all mine iniquities, but don't let me live in denial or deceiving myself, in the Name of Jesus.

Lord, create in me a clean heart, O God; and renew a right spirit within me.

Cast me not away from Thy Presence; do not let me grieve or quench the Holy Spirit. Holy Spirit be ever with me, in the Name of Jesus.

Lord, let me know the joy of Thy Salvation; and uphold me *with Thy* Spirit.

Lord, let my walk be true and let it draw even unbelievers and transgressors to You, and that sinners shall be converted unto You, in the Name of Jesus.

Deliver me from blood guiltiness~~, my own and the blood guiltiness of my ancestors, O God, in the Name of Jesus.

You are the God of my salvation: *and* my tongue shall sing aloud of Your righteousness.

O Lord, my mouth shall show forth Thy praise.

Lord, break what needs to be broken~~, The sacrifices of God *are* a broken spirit: a broken and a contrite heart, O God, Thou wilt not despise.

Rebuild my foundation in Righteousness; do good in thy good pleasure unto Zion. Lord, build the walls of my life, in the Name of Jesus.

Then, Lord, when I am properly rebuilt, You will be pleased with my sacrifices of righteousness, with burnt offering and whole burnt offering: then shall they offer bullocks upon Thine altar.

I seal these declarations across every era, age, dimension, and timeline, past, present, and future, to infinity, from the beginning to eternity. I seal them with the Blood of Jesus, and the Holy Spirit of Promise.

Any backlash because of these words, these prayers, this teaching, these decrees, and deliverance, backfire seven times, in the Name of Jesus.

AMEN.

Dear Reader

Thank you for acquiring and reading this book. May you fully see and acknowledge you Unseen Life, especially where the enemy is hiding. May you have the anointing to flush out every enemy and seek full healing and restoration to your foundation so that the Script of your life is reconciled in Christ and is the same one that you are living, to the Glory of God.

In the Name of Jesus,

Amen.

Dr. Marlene Miles

Other books by this author

AK: *The Adventures of the Agape Kid*

AMONG SOME THIEVES

Ancestral Powers https://a.co/d/9prTyFf

Backstabbers https://a.co/d/gi8iBxf

Barrenness, *Prayers Against*
https://a.co/d/feUltIs

Battlefield of Marriage, *The*

Blindsided: *Has the Old Man Bewitched You?*
https://a.co/d/5O2fLLR

Break Free from Collective Captivity

Casting Down Imaginations
https://a.co/d/1UxlLqa

Churchzilla, The Wanna-Be, Supposed-to-be Bride of Christ

Demonic Cobwebs (prayerbook)

Demonic Time Bombs

Demons Hate Questions

Devil Loves Trauma, *The*

Devil Weapons: Unforgiveness, Bitterness,…

The Devourers: Thieves of Darkness 2

Do Not Swear by the Moon

Don't Refuse Me, Lord (4 book series)
https://a.co/d/idP34LG

Dream Defilement

The Emptiers: *Thieves of Darkness, 1*
https://a.co/d/5I4n5mc

Evil Touch https://a.co/d/gSGGpS1

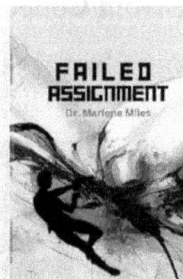

Failed Assignment https://a.co/d/3CXtjZY

Fantasy Spirit Spouse https://a.co/d/hW7oYbX

FAT Demons (The): *Breaking Demonic Curses*

The Fold (5-book series)

- The Fold (Book 1)
- Name Your Seed (Book 2)
- The Poor Attitudes of Money (3)
- Do Not Orphan Your Seed (4)
- For the Sake of the Gospel (5)
- My Sowing Journal

Gang Ups: Touch Not God's Anointed

got HEALING? Verses for Life

got LOVE? Verses for Life

got HOPE? Verses for Life

got money? https://a.co/d/g2av41N

How to Dental Assist

How to Dental Assist2: Be Productive, Not Wasteful

I Take It Back

Legacy

Let Me Have A Dollar's Worth
https://a.co/d/h8F8XgE

Level the Playing Field

Living for the NOW of God

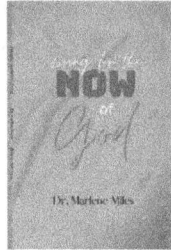

Lose My Location https://a.co/d/crD6mV9

Man Safari, *The*

Marriage Ed. Rules of Engagement &
Marriage

Made Perfect in Love

Money Hunters: Beware of Those

Money on the Altar https://a.co/d/4EqJ2Nr

Mulberry Tree https://a.co/d/9nR9rRb

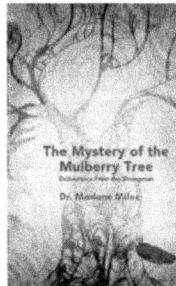

Motherboard (The) - *Soul Prosperity Series*

Name Your Seed

Occupy: *Until I Return*

Plantation Souls

Players Gonna Play

Power Money: Nine Times the Tithe
https://a.co/d/gRt41gy

The Power of Wealth *(forthcoming)*

Powers Above

Repent of Visiting Evil Altars
https://a.co/d/3n3Zjwx

The Robe, Part 1, The Lessons of Joseph

The Robe, Part II, The Lessons of Joseph

Seasons of Grief

Seasons of Waiting

Seasons of War

Second Marriage, Third--, *Any Marriage*
https://a.co/d/6m6GN4N

Sift You Like Wheat

Six Men Short: What Has Happened to all the Men?

Soul Prosperity soul prosperity series 3

https://a.co/d/5p8YvCN

Souls Captivity soul prosperity series 2

The Spirit of Poverty

StarStruck

SUNBLOCK

The Swallowers: *Thieves of Darkness*, 3

Take It Back

This Is NOT That: How to Keep Demons from Coming at You

Time Is of the Essence

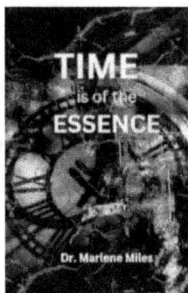

Too Many Wives: *Why You Have Lady Problems*

Tormenting Spirits   https://a.co/d/dAogEJf

Toxic Souls

Triangular Power *(series)*

- Powers Above
- SUNBLOCK

- Do Not Swear by the Moon
- STARSTRUCK

Uncontested Doom

Unguarded Hours, *The*

Unseen Life, *The*

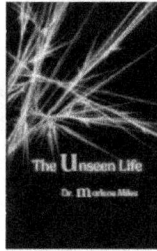

Upgrade: How to Get Out of Survival Mode

- Toxic Souls (Book 2 of series)
- Legacy (Book 3 of series)

The Wasters: *Thieves of Darkness*, Bk 2
https://a.co/d/bUvI9Jo

What Have You to Declare? What Do You Have With You from Where You've Been?

When I Was A Child, *I Prayed As a Child*

When the Devourer is Rebuked

https://a.co/d/1HVv8oq

The Wilderness Romance *(series)* This series is about conducting a Godly relationship and marriage with someone who is a Wilderness person. It is about how to recognize it and navigate through it. These books are about how not to get caught up in such.

- *The Social Wilderness*
- *The Sexual Wilderness*
- *The Spiritual Wilderness*

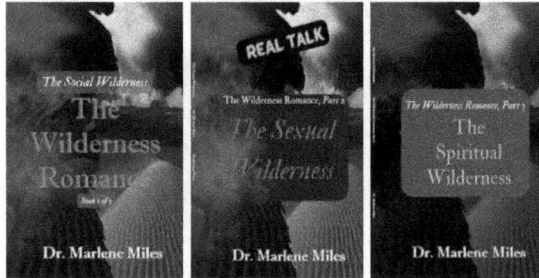

Other Series

The Fold (a series on Godly finances)
https://a.co/d/4hz3unj

Soul Prosperity Series https://a.co/d/bz2M42q

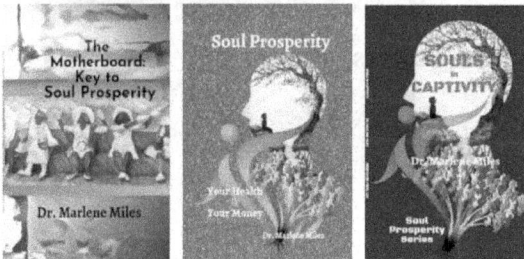

Spirit Spouse books

https://a.co/d/9VehDSo

https://a.co/d/97sKOwm

Thieves **of** **Darkness** series

Triangular Powers https://a.co/d/aUCjAWC

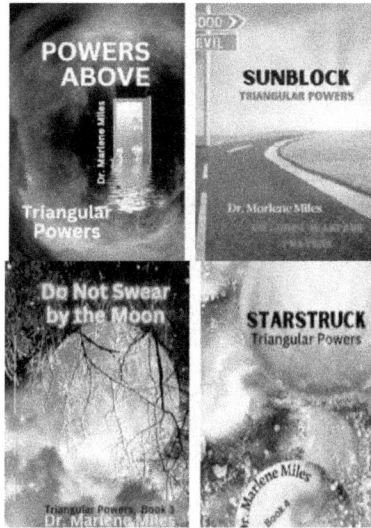

Upgrade (series) *How to Get Out of Survival Mode*
https://a.co/d/aTERhX0

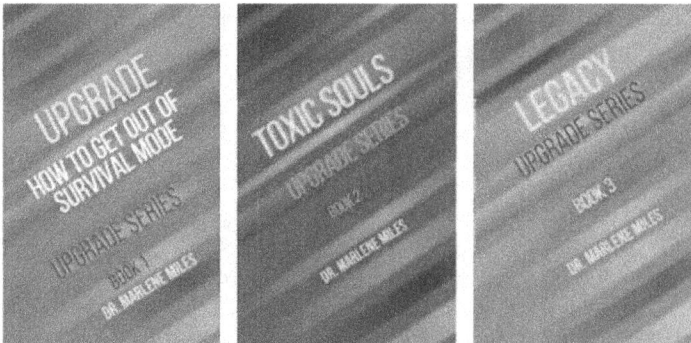

Prayer books by this author

While most books by this author have prayer points either throughout the book or at the end, there are some books that are **only** prayers. You just open up the book and pray. They are listed below:

Prayers Against Barrenness: *For Success in Business and Life*

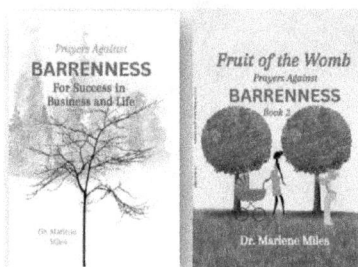

Fruit of the Womb: *Prayers Against Barrenness*

Beauty Curses, *Warfare Prayers Against*
https://a.co/d/5Xlc20M

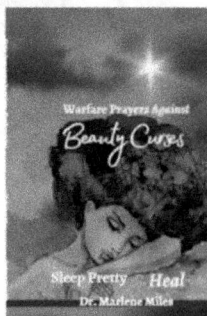

Courts of Marriage: Prayers for Marriage in the Courts of Heaven *(prayerbook)*
https://a.co/d/cNAdgAq

Courtroom Warfare @ Midnight *(prayerbook)*
https://a.co/d/5fc7Qdp

Demonic Cobwebs *(prayerbook)* https://a.co/d/fp9Oa2H

Every Evil Bird https://a.co/d/hF1kh1O

Gates of Thanksgiving

Spirits of Death, Hell & the Grave, Pass Over Me and My House https://a.co/d/d4T1sWe

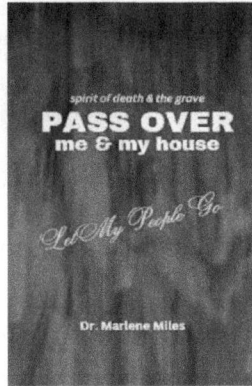

Throne of Grace: Courtroom Prayer

https://a.co/d/fNMxcM9

Warfare Prayer Against Poverty
https://a.co/d/bZ611Yu